Animals from Head to Tail

CATS FROM HEAD TO TAIL

By Tristan Noe

Gareth Stevens
PUBLISHING

Please visit our website, www.garethstevens.com. For a free color catalog of all our high-quality books, call toll free 1-800-542-2595 or fax 1-877-542-2596.

Cataloging-in-Publication Data

Names: Noe, Tristan.
Title: Cats from head to tail / Tristan Noe.
Description: New York : Gareth Stevens Publishing, 2017. | Series: Animals from head to tail | Includes index.
Identifiers: ISBN 9781482445428 (pbk.) | ISBN 9781482445367 (library bound) | ISBN 9781482445244 (6 pack)
Subjects: LCSH: Cats–Juvenile literature. | Cats–Physiology–Juvenile literature.
Classification: LCC SF445.7 N46 2017 | DDC 636.8–dc23

First Edition

Published in 2017 by
Gareth Stevens Publishing
111 East 14th Street, Suite 349
New York, NY 10003

Editor: Ryan Nagelhout
Designer: Katelyn E. Reynolds

Photo credits: Cover, p. 1 vvvita/Shutterstock.com; p. 5 Igors Rusakovs/Shutterstock.com; p. 7 Rita Kochmarjova/Shutterstock.com; p. 9 Alexandr Belous/Shutterstock.com; p. 11 Timolina/Shutterstock.com; pp. 13, 15, 24 (fur) mdmmikle/Shutterstock.com; p. 17 ThanaPhoto/Shutterstock.com; pp. 19, 24 (paw) Naviya Koomprawat/Shutterstock.com; p. 21 rokopix/Shutterstock.com; pp. 23, 24 (Manx cat) Robynrg/Shutterstock.com.

Printed in the United States of America

CPSIA compliance information: Batch #CS16GS: For further information contact Gareth Stevens, New York, New York at 1-800-542-2595.

Contents

Amazing Eyes 4

Furry Friends 12

Legs and Feet. 16

Tail or No Tail 20

Words to Know 24

Index. 24

Cats have big eyes.
They are full of color.

Most kittens
have blue eyes.

The color can change
as they grow!

Ragdoll cats
have blue eyes.

Most cats have lots of fur.
They are great to pet.

Others are hairless!

Cats have four legs.
They can move very fast.

They have pads
on their feet.
These are their paws.

Their tails
help them balance.

Some cats
have no tail at all!
These are called
Manx cats.

Words to Know

fur

Manx cat

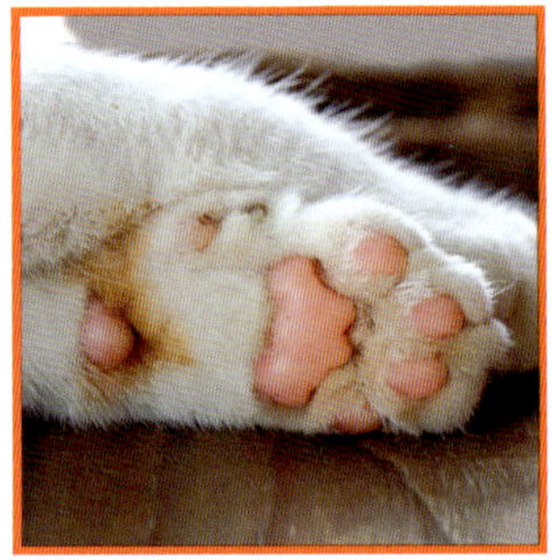

paw

Index

hairless cat 14

Manx cat 22

paws 18

Ragdoll cat 10